Sw. Solo Trumpet
Gt. Diapason 8', Flutes 8', 4', Ch to Gt.
Ch. Flute 4'
Ped. Bourdon 16'

29
Sw.
Gt. Add Flute 2', Super Octave 2'
Ped. Add Octave 8'
33
Gt.
36
(♮)
rit.
39
Gt.
a tempo
Sw.

42
45
Gt.
48
51
Sw.

Gt. Add Mix. IV
Ped. Add Diapason 16'
54
Gt.
57
slight rit.
Full Organ, no Reeds
Broader
60
63

66
69
Full Organ, with Reeds
72
Maestoso
75

Worship HYMNS FOR ORGAN.COM

Want a Brand New Carolyn Hamlin Organ Arrangement **Every Month?**

Visit *www.WorshipHymnsforOrgan.com* to learn more about Carolyn Hamlin's **Hymn of the Month** club and how to get a brand new arrangement delivered straight to your email every month.

But that's not all!

You can...

- ♪ listen to Carolyn's arrangements
- ♪ sign up for her free newsletter
- ♪ read her notes on technique and registration for different pieces
- ♪ find out more about her and the music she writes
- ♪ and so much more...

ISBN-13: 978-1-934596-75-3

50999

9 781934 596753

www.worshiphymnsfororgan.com

BGK1049
Recessional on Ode to Joy
00137270 BGK1049 $9.99

8 88680 02687 5

www.FredBock.com

EXCLUSIVELY DISTRIBUTED BY
HAL•LEONARD® CORPORATION
7777 W. BLUEMOUND RD. P.O. BOX 13819 MILWAUKEE, WI 53213